CW00642451

IMAGES OF ENGLAND

HASTINGS
REVISITED

IMAGES OF ENGLAND

HASTINGS
REVISITED

SUSAN E. KING

TEMPUS

This book is dedicated to my mother, Elsie King.

Frontispiece: St Clements church viewed from Hill Street. This, the present building, dates from the fourteenth century. The original church was sited much nearer the sea, but was destroyed by floods. To the right is The Kicking Donkey pub, and opposite is the Hole in the Wall pub.

First published 2005

Tempus Publishing Limited
The Mill, Brimscombe Port,
Stroud, Gloucestershire, GL5 2QG
www.tempus-publishing.com

© Susan E. King, 2005

The right of Susan E. King to be identified as the Author
of this work has been asserted in accordance with the
Copyrights, Designs and Patents Act 1988.

All rights reserved. No part of this book may be reprinted
or reproduced or utilised in any form or by any electronic,
mechanical or other means, now known or hereafter invented,
including photocopying and recording, or in any information
storage or retrieval system, without the permission in writing
from the Publishers.

British Library Cataloguing in Publication Data.
A catalogue record for this book is available from the British Library.

ISBN 0 7524 3543 4

Typesetting and origination by Tempus Publishing Limited.
Printed in Great Britain.

Contents

Acknowledgements

The vast majority of photographs in this book are from the extensive and impressive collection held by Hastings Library. I am indebted to Lesley Isaacs and Mick Bacon of East Sussex County Libraries for permission to reproduce them.

My thanks also go to Rowena Christodoulou, Mary Morgan, David Padgham, John Powys and Sheila Shepheard, who supplied photographs and gave me permission to use them.

Finally, I would like to thank Edward Preston for putting his immense local knowledge at my disposal whilst I was researching the book.

Every effort has been made, where possible, to trace copyright holders and secure permission to reproduce photographs.

Introduction

The jutting upper stories of medieval buildings overhang the ancient, narrow streets which lead down to the picturesque fishing beach, where the colourful vessels of the largest beach-launched fishing fleet in Great Britain line the sparkling sea. Tall, black wooden huts where the fishermen keep their nets jostle for places along the shore, interspersed with museums and heritage centres with a nautical theme. Incongruous seaside amusements and car parks are jumbled together with a thousand years of history. Traffic races along the seafront, children scream on the joy-rides, families gorge themselves on candyfloss and doughnuts, while behind it all the fishermen sell their catch straight from the boats and one of the largest flocks of herring-gulls in the country scream above the beach, helping themselves to fish-heads. This is the Hastings of today, a town with a rich heritage and a fascinating past.

The photographs gathered together in this book cover the period from the late nineteenth century to the Second World War. Many of the buildings in the photographs were in existence long before the camera was invented, and many still remain today. At street level the scene today has changed tremendously. But take a closer look. Studying these photographs from the past, and then walking the streets of Hastings (or, better still, travelling on the upper deck of a bus), and looking at the buildings at first-floor level and above, you will see that very little has altered.

The functions of some of the buildings have changed dramatically over the years. For example, the Old Town Hall and the Fishermen's church have become museums, St Mary-in-the-Castle has become an arts centre, the stables of Old Hastings House have become the Stables Theatre and the Music Hall, where Charles Dickens once gave readings from his own works, is now Yates' Wine Lodge.

Hastings is one of the most famous names in English history. Everyone knows the date of the battle, if they know nothing else. Its outcome changed our society for all time. However, the purpose of this book is not to commemorate the town's place in national history, but to open a window on its everyday life over the past hundred years or so.

At the end of the eighteenth and beginning of the nineteenth century, Hastings underwent a dramatic transformation from a tiny, ancient fishing port into an elegant and fashionable watering place. The modern concept of the seaside did not exist, and until then people did not visit the coast for pleasure. East Cliff House, overlooking the fishing beach, was the first gentleman's residence ever to be built facing the sea. Previously, the houses of wealthy people living on the coast had always been built with their backs to the sea.

When fashionable society became interested in the health and fitness value of sea air and sea bathing, everything was to change. Hastings became famous in both Great Britain and in Europe, not only for its healthy sea properties, but for its chalybeate springs which contained a high quantity of iron. It was recommended by the medical profession, and an increasing number of visitors poured into the town. To add to Hastings' popularity there was the beautiful scenery of Ecclesbourne and Fairlight Glens, where visitors could take healthy and pleasurable country walks, explore caves, buy fine silks, brandy and tobacco from the local smugglers, and enjoy of the rapidly developing fashionable social scene.

At first the visitors stayed in the Old Town, but it soon became necessary for the town to expand westwards in its new rôle. Expansion began in 1815 with the building of Wellington Place, named after the famous hero of the day, who had lived in Hastings while commanding the local troops. By 1830 Wellington Place had been extended to form Wellington Square, and the town moved steadily towards the west. At the same time, a little further to the west, the town of St Leonards was founded by James Burton and his son Decimus. Burton's St Leonards was a rare example of a town planned completely from scratch.

The shifting focus of Hastings from the Old Town to the new was fought against at the time by a great many local people. There were many stormy public meetings and protests but, as usual, those with more money and power had their way and the town began to take on its present form. The coming of the railway was a major factor in the movement to the west. Hastings station was opened in 1851, and as a result, the main post office, banks and town hall moved to new premises closer to the railway within a few decades. By the end of the nineteenth century, the Old Town had relinquished its importance, although even within living memory there have been Old Towners who have seldom set foot in the newer part of Hastings except to go to the post office. The towns of Hastings and St Leonards, initially rivals, ultimately merged in 1869.

In the early years of photography there were sometimes skilled amateur photographers who had a special interest in recording a town, an area, or a way of life. Times were changing, and they wanted to capture for posterity a pictorial record of things they feared would disappear within a few years. Hastings was lucky to have such a man in George Woods, who came to live in the town in the late 1880s and took thousands of superb photographs of the fishing industry and many other aspects of late Victorian life. A great many of his photographs survive, some of which are reproduced in this book. They, and the other photographs gathered here, portray a vivid impression of what it was like to live in Hastings at the time, and in many instances are the only known visual record of what were once familiar things.

Susan E. King
March 2005

one

The Fishing
Community

NET HOUSES AND HARBOUR FROM EAST HILL, HASTINGS. (30)

Packing the fish into boxes and barrels at the open-air wholesale Fishmarket. The handcart is probably an ice cart. The Hastings Fishmarket handled enormous quantities of fish for several decades, although by the time this photograph was taken in the 1890s the industry was already slipping into a decline that continued right up until the First World War.

Opposite above: Hastings stade (fishing beach) in the 1870s, before the harbour arm was built. A coasting brig is being unloaded directly onto the beach by a team of men with horses and carts. Larger vessels such as this
were run onto the shore at high tide, where they would wait until low tide to be unloaded. There were far more net shops at this time, occupying a longer stretch of beach than they do today.

Opposite below: The stade showing the horse capstans used to wind the boats up the beach, with the circular tracks made by the horses walking round. This picture was taken shortly after 1933 when the boating lake was built, but before 1937/38 when the horse capstans began to be replaced by power winches. At the bottom is the Fishermen's church, built in 1853.

The large piece of machinery on the left is an ice-flaking machine. The vast quantities of ice used to pack the fish were made in the ice-house in Rock-a-Nore Road. The small boy probably feels very grown-up helping his father.

Opposite above: Hastings Fishmarket in the 1890s. Looking at this busy scene it is difficult to imagine that the industry had already declined from its hey-day in the mid-nineteenth century. This was mainly due to the railways making it easy to transport and sell fish from the east coast to Hastings. Between the two pubs (the Queens Head and the Jolly Fisherman) are the premises of the Kent & Sussex Pure Ice Co.

Opposite below: The round (retail) Fishmarket, was built by Hastings Borough Council in 1870 at the bottom of the High Street. It was demolished in 1928 to make way for a turning circle for trolleybuses. The area is now a car park. The wooden structure is the storm signalling tower, and behind it can be seen the Queens Head Hotel.

Old Town women counting herrings into baskets on the beach opposite East Beach Street, in the 1890s. This was traditionally women's work, and they counted herrings by the warp. Four herrings = one warp, thirty warps = a 'long hundred' (120 fish).

Opposite above: Buying fish from fish barrows in the 1890s. Most of the retail selling was done by fish stalls and fish barrows. Fish barrows were pushed all across the town, each seller having regular routes which commonly stayed in the same families for generations.

Opposite below: A yoke was a useful piece of equipment for those hawking their wares around the town. It took most of the weight and prevented the baskets from hitting the wearer's knees. This photograph was taken in Priory Road before the Second World War. The man looks like a fisherman, but what exactly is he selling? Tantalisingly, even a hand-lens does not quite reveal the goods in the baskets.

East Beach Street in the 1890s. Fish boxes and barrels can be seen stored under the houses on the left and piled in the street.

A quiet moment amongst the net shops. These unique wooden buildings are called shops because the fishermen used them as workshops as well as for storage of nets, ropes and sails. They are exceptionally tall and narrow in order to save space on the beach. The boat on the left has a lute stern, a design which ensures that waves will break harmlessly beneath the boat when it is lying in the surf. On the right a line of fish hangs out to dry.

These net shops in East Beach Street had already started to change their role by the time this photograph was taken, around 1910. To the right of centre is W. Dine & Sons, barbers. To the extreme left is a newsagent.

Punts on the stade, *c.* 1890. The fisherman is holding a shrimp trawl. Behind can be seen some of the many pubs in the Old Town, including The Rising Sun, The Pelican and The Queens Head, as well as Adam's Refreshment Rooms.

James Gallop, also known as 'Jimmy Sole', is seen here in 1913 making some extra income selling seashells to tourists. Many of the fishermen had, and still have, nicknames. This is partly fun, partly useful in a tight-knit community where many intermarriages result in a lot of people with the same names.

A wide variety of baskets are needed by a fishing community, and basket makers also make lobster pots. This man appears to be attaching long handles to the baskets. His top hat adds a flamboyant touch.

A typical Hastings fisherman photographed in 1905. This is Mr Young in his sou'wester and canvas smock. The fishermen boiled their smocks in tanning fluid, together with the sails, ropes and nets, at the Tan House at Rock-a-Nore. The tanning fluid preserved them and gave them their traditional red ochre colour. As a result, the Hastings fishermen earned their nickname 'Tanfrocks'.

The Winkle Club was formed by a group of fishermen in 1899 to raise money to give the poor children in the Old Town a Christmas tea and a show. The parties continued annually until the 1970s, and are remembered with great affection by many Old Towners. Seated in the centre is Mr E.J. Breeds, with the winkle at his feet, *c.* 1927.

Up until the Second World War, the children were accompanied by the Winkle Club Band from their assembly point at the Fishmarket to the Rock-a-Nore Drill Hall, where the parties were held. Mrs Sarah Breeds (in the white blouse) stands to the left of the drummer. Behind them is the London Trader pub, 1927

Above: A group of fishermen mend their nets by a horse capstan. The long pole that one man rests his foot on is a capstan bar. This is placed in the capstan when a boat is ready to be wound up the beach. The boat is attached to the capstan wire, and the horse is attached to the capstan bar and walks round in a circle. In the background (right) is the Tan House. This picture was taken by local photographer George Woods, around 1890.

Right: Fishermen at the net shops in the 1890s. In the early days Hastings made all its own nets, but by the 1850s most nets were coming from Dorset. However, net-making in the Old Town continued on a minor scale, not only for the fishing fleet but for other uses such as garden net and for poaching.

Above: Men making nets, around the 1890s, while others relax and read the newspaper outside the premises of T. Quick, boot maker. The notice chalked on the first floor door reads, 'Prawn nets sold here'.

Right: Mending the nets. This is another carefully posed photograph taken by George Woods in the 1890s. Woods and his camera became very well known in the town and the fishermen were happy to pose for him.

Opposite above: A group of fishermen with their net by a punt, *c.* 1910. Up until the Second World War, punts were often used for taking holiday-makers on trips during the summer, and for fishing during the winter.

Opposite below: Lifting a boat ashore, *c.* 1890. This is the *Weg*, owned by 'Mackerel' Gallop. The co-operation needed to do jobs like this is one of the things which has formed the strength and the closeness of the fishing community.

A coaster being unloaded on the beach in the 1870s. In the foreground are the remains of the Elizabethan harbour, exposed by storms. There was a harbour in the late Middle Ages which was destroyed around 1560. Many efforts were made to rebuild it over the next hundred years, but the attempt was finally abandoned.

An attempt to build a harbour in 1896 ran into constant trouble. The project was extremely contentious, nobody wanted to finance it, and the harbour promoters eventually ran out of funds. However, they did manage to build the harbour arm which still remains today. Lord Dufferin laid the stone at the further end in 1897, and this photograph shows the harbour train bringing back the dignitaries after the ceremony.

The wreck of the *Nerissa*, run aground at Castle Rocks in 1891 after being caught in a terrible storm off Beachy Head. The enormous waves which constantly struck the vessel caused her to leak, and the pumps were unworkable. The master, Mr D. Jenkins, and crew were saved. Afterwards, Mr Jenkins, a highly experienced seaman, said that the conditions were the worst he had ever encountered.

The Victorian lifeboat house was built in 1882 on the site of the old Custom House in East Parade, replacing an earlier lifeboat house at Rock-a-Nore. Curiously, Hastings Borough Council built a boating lake for tourists between the lifeboat house and the sea, thus hindering the launch of the lifeboat. The new lifeboat house was built in 1949 and this splendid Victorian building was demolished ten years later.

The Hastings lifeboat, *Charles Arkoll II*, which served for thirty years between 1901 and 1931. She and her predecessor were named after a locally-born man who became mayor of Maidstone, and left £2,000 in his will for the provision of lifeboat facilities in his home town.

The first Hastings motor lifeboat, the *Cyril & Lilian Bishop*, seen here in 1939, replaced the *Charles Arkoll II* in 1931. She was built by J. Samuel White & Co. of Cowes, Isle of Wight, and was one of the new self-righting types. During the Second World War, she took part in the Dunkirk evacuation. She served at Hastings until 1950, and was replaced by the *M.T.C.*, also built at Cowes.

two

Tourism

Hastings Castle broods on top of an enormous West Hill, whose size owes more to the artist's imagination than to reality, *c.* 1830. Beneath are Pelham Crescent, with St Mary-in-the-Castle in the centre, and Breeds Place. Part of the castle was knocked down in the 1820s to make space to build them.

Getting out to the pleasure boats was a hazardous operation for early visitors. Boatmen had to carry the passengers out to the vessels, and this cartoon comes pretty close to the truth.

Marine Parade in 1823. A few early bathing machines appear on the beach. These were listed amongst the town's attractions in the very first *Hastings Guide*, published 1794. In those early days, bathers were dipped into the sea by robust bathing men and women. It was all a very sober business, undergone for health rather than pleasure.

East Parade, around 1910, with an array of horse-drawn vehicles ready to take visitors on trips around the town. There appear to be no takers amongst these visitors. A driver reads the papers and a horse feeds from his nosebag while waiting.

Above: West Hill Lift was the first of the town's two lifts to be built, taking visitors up the hill to the castle. This photograph was taken soon after the lift was opened in 1891. The original Victorian cars are still in use today.

Right: An early photograph showing several ladies in fashionable crinolines visiting the ruins of the collegiate church of St Mary in Hastings Castle, *c.* 1865. It is possible that there was a church here in Saxon times.

Left: East Hill Lift was built in 1902. It is believed to be the steepest in Britain, and was initially worked by water – alternately emptying and filling water-tanks, built into the cars, raised and lowered them by gravity. Arriving at the top visitors could enjoy a ramble through the pretty coastal glens.

Below: Taking refreshment at the tea-place at the top of Fairlight Glen, around the turn of the century. A smartly dressed waitress stands by the door. The Dripping Well close by was a well-known tourist spot.

Left: This early photograph shows a lady and gentleman enjoying the romantic setting at Lovers' Seat, near Fairlight Glen, *c.* 1860. A legend grew up about a pair of star-crossed lovers at this popular spot, which has now fallen into the sea.

Below: The interior of St Mary-in-the-Castle, showing its circular auditorium with a huge domed roof and seating for 500 people, *c.* 1860. Other unusual features of the church include the natural spring which rises up inside it, the former immersion font, and the catacombs.

Left: The graceful Ionic portico of St Mary's is the focal point of Pelham Crescent. St Mary's was designed by Joseph Kay and built between 1824 and 1828. Last used as a church in 1970, it became derelict and was rescued from the threat of demolition by The Friends of St Mary-in-the-Castle, who worked tirelessly for its restoration, and turned it into an Arts Centre.

Below: Wellington Square was the first part of the modern town centre to be built. On the left is the Castle Hotel, opened in 1817. The gardens in the centre were originally for the use of residents only. When this photograph was taken in the 1930s, the Square had become a terminus for country buses. The elegant Castle Hotel was demolished in 1966.

176. THE BEACH, HASTINGS. —JUDGES'

An elegantly dressed lady is assisted down the steps as passengers disembark from the *New Albertine*, *c.* 1910. The *New Albertine* was built in Hastings in 1891 and was one of the two largest beach-launched pleasure yachts in Britain. The other was also built in Hastings and worked at Eastbourne.

Opposite above: The Queens Hotel with the pleasure yachts beached outside by Harold Place, 1904. The two cupolas have now gone. The Queens was built on the former America Ground and opened in 1862. Its closure was a dramatic result of the 1987 hurricane. After a long period of doubt and several owners, it has now been restored and developed as private flats.

Opposite below: A crowded summer's day, perhaps August Bank Holiday, on the seafront at Denmark Place, *c.* 1900. Passengers swarm aboard the two big pleasure yachts, the *New Albertine* and the *New Skylark*. On the left, advertising Bovril, is the Carlisle Hotel.

The crew of the first *Albertine* in the 1880s. From left to right are: -?-, 'Prigsy' Ball, 'Bellsie' Mitchell and Thomas Hugh. Many local fishermen earned extra money in the summer working on the pleasure boats, either the big yachts, the paddle steamers, or the many small craft taking holiday-makers for trips.

The big pleasure yachts, like the fishing boats, were wound up the beach by a horse winch, as seen in this photograph taken around 1890. The horses were owned by Hastings Borough Council. The horses' other job, when they were not winding up boats, was pulling the town's dust-carts.

THE YACHTS AT HASTINGS

Left: The *New Albertine* on the beach outside the Queens Hotel, *c.* 1910. She was a major tourist attraction and continued to provide pleasure trips until 1924. After giving pleasure to thousands of visitors for over thirty years, she was sold in 1927 and spent her final days in the Newhaven area as a working boat.

Below: One of P & A Campbell's paddle steamers operating from Hastings Pier, *c.* 1925. As well as local trips there were longer ones to Brighton, Folkestone and Boulogne. Many of these paddle steamers went over to Dunkirk during the Second World War.

A fortune-teller plying her trade outside the Queens Hotel. For a penny the canary in the cage would pick a card and the woman, who wore a brightly coloured headscarf and earrings and was said to be Russian, would tell the customer's fortune. To the right, a small boat has been pulled far up into Harold Place. This photograph was taken by George Woods in the 1890s.

The German submarine *U118* was washed ashore at Denmark Place in 1919 whilst being towed to France as one of the spoils of war. It became a great attraction for townsfolk and tourists alike, until it was eventually scrapped. In the foreground is one of the many little craft taking tourists for trips, and to the left is the *New Albertine*.

Bathing machines at the water's edge by Carlisle Parade, *c.* 1890. One of the horses which drew the bathing machines down to the sea is just visible in the centre of the photograph. Men and women were segregated to different bathing areas. In 1901 nearby Bexhill was the first resort in Britain to permit mixed bathing.

Carlisle Parade just before the tramlines were laid. A boot-black awaits customers besides the pavement, and behind him a goat rests contentedly on the road, ready to draw a goat-cart for child visitors. The man in the white jacket is also looking for customers for his wares. (Broderick, 1905).

An early photographer at work photographing a family group, *c.* 1900. The man on the left is holding a screen up to cut out the glare of the sun. It looks as if the photographer is about to use his hat for a similar purpose.

In the early twentieth century people always dressed impeccably, even for the beach, but this group, taken around 1915, may have been celebrating a special occasion, possibly the wedding anniversary of the older couple in the centre. There is an absence of young men, who were perhaps away at the Front during the First World War. Note the careful posing to reveal the photographer's premises between the ladies in the back row.

A delightfully informal picture taken in 1915 for the local newspaper. 'We have a dip every morning and thoroughly enjoy it' wrote Miss Harborne, one of the 'mermaids', to her father in Bow. Hastings was a popular venue for works and other group outings from London.

An elderly couple selling shells from their fine display, *c.* 1905. Hastings beach has never been a good place for shells as the shingle breaks them up, so shells were imported from foreign parts to be sold to tourists.

Exquisite sand-paintings of cathedrals and other places of interest were a well-loved attraction. However, this was only allowed on designated parts of the beach and those who attempted it elsewhere were fined. This pitch was opposite Robertson Street in 1932. The art still continues to this day.

The bandstand at White Rock, c. 1905. Erected in 1895, the White Rock Baths were opened in 1874, and built under the parade which was extended to form the roof. A sign points to the gentlemen's bath, which was separate from the ladies' bath, and was the largest covered bath in Great Britain.

Hastings Pier, around 1890, with one of the paddle-steamers which ran regularly from the end. Opened in 1872, the pier is seen here in its original elegance. The Pavilion was the only building on the pier for the first thirty-six years, the original conception of piers being to provide people with a novel and healthy promenade from which they could also get a different view of the town.

This photograph from around 1890 must have been taken as soon as the pier opened in the morning, to capture it without any visitors. Around the wonderful Victorian turnstile an array of posters advertise the delights of the pier; paddle-steamers, concerts and artistes. Along the side of the pier can be seen the cast-iron seats that ran along its entire 900ft length.

The Pavilion at the end of the pier, built in the Moorish style, around 1905. The interior was equally ornate, with a very eastern appearance. The theatre could seat 700 people.

Crowds enjoying a band concert, one of the delights of a summer's evening on the promenade. The tramlines date this photograph to after 1905. The boy speeding along on his bicycle runs the risk of getting stuck in them, a common hazard of the time.

Hastings Pier, around 1910. More structures have been put up, including the shore-end pavilion and 'The joywheel, where laughter reigns supreme'. Up to 30,000 people would pass through the turnstiles on a busy bank holiday.

The shore end of the pier looks very different in this photograph, taken a few years later between 1914, when the new bandstand was opened, and 1917 when the ornate sea-end pavilion burnt down. The 'modern' bandstand with its encircling shelters and kiosks was intended to update the town's image.

Onlookers crowd the beach to watch in awe at the fire which destroyed the magnificent sea-end pavilion in 1917. Some soldiers had attended a concert the night before, and it was believed that the fire was started by the careless disposal of a cigarette butt in the pavilion. Its replacement was built in the Art Deco style in the 1920s.

Well-loved local character Biddy (Alfred) Stonham, known as Biddy the Tubman, pretends to take pot-shots at his audience with his oar. Biddy was the most famous, and the last, of several tubmen who performed antics for the amusement of holiday-makers, while their assistants collected money from the crowd.

Bath-chair men pulling convalescent or aged passengers by Eversfield Place. For well over a hundred years the sick, the convalescent, and others in search of good health brought a lot of income to the town. Bath chairs continued to be available for hire right up until the Second World War.

A milkman pushes a hand-cart containing a churn past Queen Victoria's statue in Warrior Square, c. 1905. Warrior Square was laid out in the early 1860s, and was said to be 'the largest and finest square in England'.

East Ascent, St Leonards on Sea

James Burton's new town of St Leonards, soon after it was built, *c.* 1830. On the left are the Assembly Rooms, and next to them is East Villa. A carriage is bringing some fashionable visitors to the main entrance of the Royal Victoria Hotel. Since visitors no longer pass between the Assembly Rooms and the hotel, the hotel's main entrance now faces the sea. The Assembly Rooms have become the Masonic Hall.

Two ladies walk up the hill past South Lodge, the entrance to St Leonard's Gardens, *c.* 1905. The gardens were originally owned by James Burton's family and public admission was by subscription.

The Archway, seen here around 1890, marked the eastern boundary of St Leonards, and was one of the first structures of the new town to be built. It was demolished in 1895 to widen the road. There was much public opposition to its demolition, and one morning people woke up to find that it had been secretly demolished by the borough council in the night.

A well-dressed couple relax on a bench outside Nos 15-21 Marina, while the horse-drawn Queen's Laundry van trots briskly by, c. 1905. On the left is the entrance to the shops in South Colonnade.

The Lower Parade shortly after it was opened in the 1930s. As originally designed, the seaward side could be completely closed by sliding glass windows. These were seldom used, and eventually rusted up and were removed.

The Sun Lounge (now the Marina Pavilion), and Marine Court were both built in 1937 by Borough Engineer Sidney Little, 'The Concrete King'. The controversial Marine Court was designed to look like an ocean-going liner and met with a lot of local opposition.

Bathing cabins by St Leonards Pier, *c.* 1910. Hastings is said to have been the first resort in the country to have bathing cabins, a continental idea introduced in 1906 by Mr Ben Laws. They proved to be very popular and rapidly replaced the old-fashioned bathing machines.

St Leonards Pier and a remarkably empty promenade, *c.* 1900. An elderly gentleman in a bath chair is taking the air. A lady accompanies another invalid in a bath chair by the railings. Perhaps they are taking an early morning constitutional before breakfast.

A summer's day on St Leonards Pier in 1905, with traditional pier amusements. A family enjoys the nameplate machine (right). Next to it stands a weighing machine, and on the opposite side of the pier is a punchball.

St Leonards bathing pool in the 1930s. Still fondly remembered by many people, it was built to Olympic standards. Once the pride and joy of the town, it was later turned into a holiday camp and eventually became a derelict eyesore, finally being demolished in 1993.

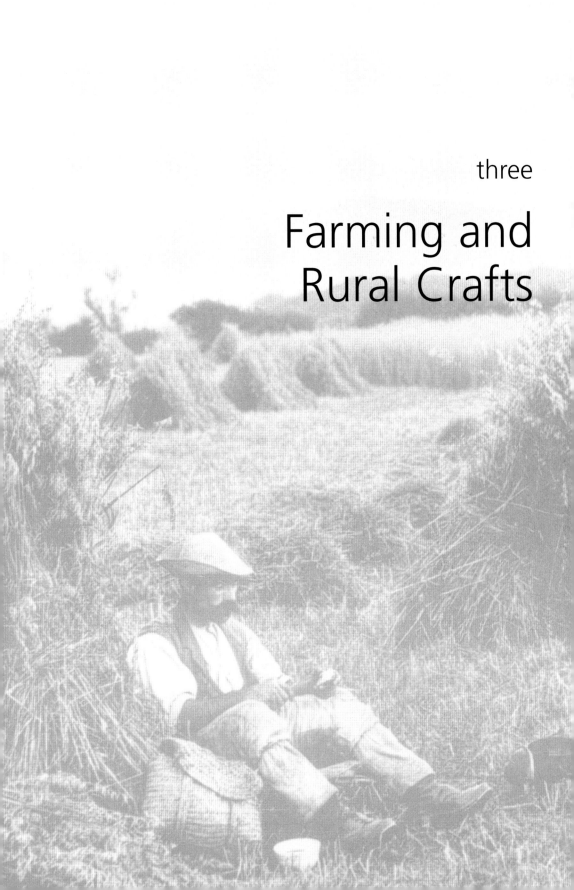

three

Farming and
Rural Crafts

An idyllic scene at Great Ridge Farm before the war. The small attached cottage at the far end (on the right) housed two farm workers. Behind it is the dairy room, with its cool, north-facing window. Built in 1658, the main buildings look the same today, though the barn is now a private house and the duck pond is a car park.

Opposite above: Ploughing with an ox-team at the turn of the twentieth century. A man with a stick turns the beasts. A four-ox team needed a large space in which to turn. While they paused, the ploughman would take the opportunity to scrape the share.

Opposite below: A sturdy pair of oxen draws a two-wheeled cart, *c.* 1900. Sussex was the last county to use oxen (castrated cattle) as draft animals. There are still some people who can remember ox-teams being a common sight. The oxen were put to work at about two-and-a-half years old, and sent to market for beef when they reached seven.

Discing with a horse-team to break up the soil, *c.* 1900. The horses are in fine condition, their coats gleaming in the sunshine. The horseman has to be a sensitive and intelligent man, with a good rapport with his animals.

Opposite above: Sheep-washing to guard against blow-fly and other parasites, *c.* 1900. In the background sheep from the flock are pushed into the water against the current. The man standing on the brink thrusts them under as they swim along, with a long stick shaped like a crutch. When the wool becomes saturated, the men in the foreground, who have the wettest part of the job, assist them out.

Opposite below: Cutting the hay on Mr Smith's farm at Tile Kiln between the wars. After the hay was cut, the swathes were turned by hand and fluffed up until they dried. When dry, they were raked up into windrows.

Once all the green had gone out of the hay and it was thoroughly dry it was loaded onto the carts. The man on the left holds a long-handled drag rake. There were many different regional variations of hay-rakes, and their design was according to what suited the land of the area. The rake in the photograph, with its many tines and braced head, was well suited to gathering long, luxuriant hay from the fertile lowlands. Hay wains, too, had regional variations, both in shape and in the colours in which they were painted; Red for the wheels and undercarriage and blue for the body was fairly common.

Everyone who could turned out to help at this very busy time. Some of the women, seen here around 1890, wear sunbonnets to keep the sun off their necks and prevent sunstroke while they are working. Once finished, this stack would have been thatched with straw or rushes.

Cider making was an important part of the farmer's year. The man on the extreme right of this photograph from around 1890 shovels up the apples from the tub into the cider mill, where the two grinders chop them up ready for the cider press on the left. The farmer is on the left of the press.

Opposite above: A farm labourer harvests the crop with a sickle, while another binds the sheaves. The stooks behind them are formed by propping two sheaves firmly up against each other and piling six or eight more around them. This and the following photograph was taken in Fairlight, *c.* 1890.

Opposite below: Sitting in the shade of a stook, a farm labourer enjoys his well-earned *nammit* (lunch). The stooked sheaves will be left to dry before being stacked in ricks in the yard.

Above: There were three windmills on the West Hill in the mid-nineteenth century. This is the Priory Road windmill, seen here in 1860 when it was the only one left. It was demolished in 1874. The building with the chimney is the steam mill which was built in 1849.

Right: Many local people will remember Draper's Mill at Silverhill. It was last worked in 1941, before falling into dereliction until it was demolished in 1966. The millstones can still be seen forming part of a nearby garden wall in Windmill Road.

Opposite above: Mr T. Furminger's smithy at St Leonards Green, *c.* 1900. At that time there were so many horses to be shod that four men could hardly keep up with the work. As well as shoeing horses blacksmiths did a wide variety of jobs, including repairing farm tools and equipment and putting metal tyres on wooden wheels. Part of the premises was used by Jesse Smith, fly proprietor (a fly was a light carriage, the fore-runner of a taxi-cab).

Opposite below: Another smithy, with blacksmiths at work, *c.* 1890. One shapes an iron strip into a horseshoe on the anvil. An enormous pair of bellows hangs on the wall. The array of tongs by the forge was used for gripping every size and shape of hot metal. The smithy was a magnet for local youths, who gathered to watch the sparks fly as the blacksmiths worked.

Above: Tree felling on the Beauport Park estate at the turn of the twentieth century. A canvas shelter has been erected for the woodmen, and a team of horses waits to transport the timber. Only the most powerful horses could pull the extremely heavy timber-wagons. Every part of the tree was used. Oak bark would be stripped and sold for tanning.

Left: A local besom-maker chopping clean the base of the broom head before inserting the handle, *c.* 1890. Many besom-makers (or 'broom squires') lived and worked in the woods during the summer, where their raw materials were on hand.

Opposite: A basket-maker and his assistant at work, *c.* 1890. In front is a bundle of withies (young willow shoots). A wide assortment of their finished wares hangs above them. Baskets were used for hop picking, harvesting and transporting a wide range of farm produce and seafood until the late 1950s, when cardboard boxes took over.

Charcoal burning was an important craft in this area, supplying the Wealden iron industry with fuel; it gives a very intense heat, twice that of wood. Here a burn has just been completed. A man stands with a bucket of water to extinguish the kiln, while a man with a spade is ready to open it up.

The kiln has been opened and the charcoal burner spreads out the finished charcoal with a rake. It was then sorted and sifted ready for use. As it was essential to watch the kilns twenty-four hours a day, the charcoal burner and his family lived in the simple shelter in the background. These two photographs were taken around 1890, but methods continued unchanged up until the Second World War.

four

Shops and Streets

Right: A splendid display of poultry outside the premises of Charles Crouch, butcher and poulterer, at Nos 10–11 Alpine Road, in 1906. The butcher on the left holds a long pole for getting down the birds.

Below: A later photograph of the smithy at St Leonards Green (seen in the previous chapter), taken around 1910. On the right, Mr Furminger has opened a greengrocer's, and Jesse Smith has opened a butcher's shop.

Opposite above: Fairlight Farm Dairy at No. 40 Whitefriars Road, in 1913. The proprietor, Mr H.P. Linch, stands in the doorway. The boy in the centre wears a yoke to carry two wooden tubs, and two female assistants or family members look out of the window.

Opposite below: A delivery man from Mount Pleasant Dairy poses proudly by his trade bicycle, *c.* 1920. The proprietor is again Mr H.P. Linch.

Left: W. Vennall, fishmonger and herring curer, All Saints Street, *c.* 1910. A row of fish, probably herrings, hangs in the window. The building dates from around 1450. The adjoining house is of similar date but the timber-framing has been plastered over to update it.

Below: All Saints Street shortly after the fifteenth-century houses had been restored in the 1930s. A donkey is being led up the street, and there is no traffic in evidence, but a street sign has already made its appearance – under the Swan Vestas poster.

TUDOR HOUSES, ALL SAINTS' STREET, HASTINGS, A.D. 1450.

Right: Frank Pelham, chemist, at the bottom of the High Street. Note the spelling, 'chymist', on the tiles beneath the window, indicating that this is older than the sign above the shop. This splendid shop front has fortunately been preserved in all its glory. The Ilford advertisement suggests the photograph was taken in the 1950s.

Below: The High Street in the 1930s. The post office is on the left, and next to it, at the edge of the picture, is the old customs house. Railings have been put up on the high pavement. There is a corresponding high pavement on the right side of All Saints Street, running parallel to this, an indication that the Old Town is built in a river valley.

HIGH STREET, HASTINGS.

Above: Time for a chat in George Street, around the 1930s. On the left is Stoakes & Carey, boot and shoe shop. This is now the Pump House pub. The notice high on the wall advertises Ernest Avery & Co. drapers.

Right: George Street was the first extension of the Old Town to be built when Hastings developed as a resort. It was constructed around 1811 and became the town's shopping centre for the next fifty years. The shop on the right has invested in a row of gas-lights, and tradesmen's carts fill the road, *c.* 1900.

Opposite above: East Beach Street in 1935. These shops, selling beach trays, cups of tea, ice cream, postcards and souvenirs, were originally net shops. Look back at the photograph at the top of page 17 to see what they looked like in the 1890s.

Opposite below: East Parade in the 1900s. The grocer's in the centre also offers teas. Next door is a hairdressing salon. The building next to the Rising Sun pub, with the domed roof, is the lower lighthouse. Two unaccompanied dogs saunter in the road and the boy in the foreground leads a very small puppy.

The much loved Albert Memorial awaits the fitting of its clock. Already people are finding it an agreeable place to loiter and meet old acquaintances. Built in 1862/63, the Memorial was the central point of Hastings for the next 110 years. The building with the central pediment was the Music Hall, where Charles Dickens gave a public reading the year before the Memorial was built.

The lack of crowds and traffic in this early morning photograph give the Memorial and Harold Place an air of elegant grandeur, *c.* 1880. At its base a few early risers linger in the sunshine. The building on the left is the York Hotel, closed in 1965 and now demolished.

The flags are out for a special occasion and the horse-bus is crowded with passengers in this photograph, taken around 1890. The Memorial area, situated at an important crossroads, was the first place in Hastings to have street lighting.

The unusual vantage point chosen by the unknown photographer was probably a window of the Public Hall, c. 1953. The Memorial was demolished in 1973, yet controversy still rages about the mysterious circumstances of its demise. Despite being gone for over thirty years, the area is still known unofficially as 'the Memorial'.

Horse-drawn removal vans are lined up alongside removal men and other staff posing outside Tapner & Woodman's Furniture Depository in Waterworks Road, around 1905, before the premises suffered a disastrous fire.

A typical seaside shop at Denmark Place, c. 1950. Holiday-makers look at postcards and the array of buckets, spades, shrimping nets, and other delights on display. The signs above advertise ice creams, Hastings rock and cups of tea.

Grand Parade at the turn of the twentieth century. Beneath Eversfield Mansions Boarding Establishment is Burton's Library. There were a great many private circulating libraries in the town. The earliest was opened by John Stell in the Old Town in 1788.

Burton's new town of St Leonards included the purpose-built shops of South Colonnade, built in 1829, seen here in 1905. Thomas and Martha Mawle opened the first grocer's shop, and their daughter was the first child to be born in St Leonards. James Burton presented the parents with a silver tea-service to mark the event.

A lady contemplates a purchase from the flower-seller's stall on its regular pitch outside the Capital & Counties Bank (later the Midland) at the bottom of London Road, 1905.

A coal merchant making a delivery, c. 1910. A man with a barrow waits to take the coal to the customer's house. The gigantic feathered hooves of the shire horse can be seen beneath the cart.

A sunny day in Bohemia Road, 1905. All the shops have their sun blinds out. The blinds were also pulled out on rainy days, so that potential customers could linger in the dry while window-shopping. The post office has only very recently closed.

Bohemia Road, *c.* 1905. The area does not look too different today, and there are many relics of these shop fronts of a hundred years ago still to be found by the observant.

A horse-bus goes past Silverhill Junction and the Rainbow Temperance Hotel, c. 1905. The stone eagles on the gateposts of Cremer House are still there today. This scene dates from before the roads were tarmacked, as can be seen from the rutted surface. A small dog waits for his owner outside the tobacconist's shop.

Silverhill Junction from Sedlescombe Road South. The Rainbow Hotel and shops on the right were demolished shortly after this photograph was taken, c. 1910. On the opposite corner is Sayer's Drapery Store, and in the distance can be seen the Welcome Stranger pub and the spire of St Luke's church.

five

Childhood

Drawing the household's water from the East Well, in the 1890s. This natural spring was the only source of fresh water for many families. All children were expected to help in the home, and fetching the water was a task often allocated to them.

Poor children returning from the West Hill Soup Kitchen in 1909. There was a lot of poverty, especially in the Old Town, between the 1880s and the First World War. Any handy household receptacles were taken along to one of the soup kitchens, which operated during the winters in many parts of the town.

Above: The Ore Penny Dinners for poor children, *c.* 1900. Unemployment meant that some families were so poverty-stricken that the children went for a day or two without food. Schoolteachers would give such children a penny token from the fund, which they could then exchange for a meal.

Below: Children playing in All Saints Street near the Alma Tavern, free from the oppression of modern-day traffic, *c.* 1910. There are as yet no railings along the high pavement.

Youngsters dancing to the music of a barrel organ outside the Dolphin Inn, *c.* 1910. Judging by the row of ladies standing against the wall, it is probably an organised event, and the girls appear to be in a square set. Country dancing was having a revival at this time, due to Cecil Sharp and the English Folk Dance and Song Society.

The delights of a wave-cut platform and its rock pools, teeming with life, are timeless. Visitors and local children alike enjoy a summer's day by the sea's edge, *c.* 1910.

A row of little girls line up for the camera at Ore village fête, before sampling the fun of the swingboats, the steam-driven carousel, and the sideshows in Goddens Field, Rock Lane, *c.* 1900. In the distance can be seen the White Mill at Fairlight Down.

Class three at All Saint's School, *c.* 1925. The children wrote on slates with slate pencils. The slates were simply wiped clean with a damp sponge after use, and then were ready to be used again. If a child did not go to school, the School Board man would come round to the home and ask why.

Mary Magdalen School, known as 'The Penny School', *c.* 1915. The pupils had to bring a penny per week to pay for their education.

The boys of Mount Pleasant School football team before the First World War. But where is the ornate building behind them?

Clive Vale School orchestra at the turn of the century. The music teacher stands on the left, the headmaster on the right. The orchestra appears to be composed entirely of violins and violas.

Hurst Court Preparatory School, the Ridge, *c.* 1908. There were many high-class private schools for both boarders and day pupils in Hastings and St Leonards. The parents of many of the pupils lived abroad and sent their children back to England to be educated.

Hastings Grammar School was originally founded in 1878. This new building opened in 1883 at the top of Nelson Road by the railway line. The boys could enjoy watching the passing steam trains out of the classroom windows to relieve the monotony of lessons.

Remove A at Hastings Grammar School in 1934. Some boys were fee-paying pupils, but most were scholarship boys from the local elementary schools. Scholarships were provided by the Local Education Authority for those who passed the requisite exam, the forerunner of the 11-plus. At this time the school-leaving age was fourteen, but a condition of the scholarship was that pupils remained at school until aged sixteen.

A fine action shot of boys playing in a six-a-side football match, cheered on by a large crowd of their schoolfellows outside Hastings Grammar School, 1958.

The Lower Fifth at Hastings and St Leonards Ladies College, Dane Road, in 1951, the year the school closed. From left to right, back row: Hope Gosse, Diana Ross-Slater, Marian Daws, Margaret Parkman, Jane Surridge. Front row: Cynthia Arscott, Sheila Carr, Joan Carpenter, Margaret Cruttenden, Angela Ferraro.

Boys Life Brigade, 1st Hastings Company Cadets, 1917. At that time the Boys' Brigade was run on military lines. One boy wears an ordinary cap, possibly because he is a new recruit.

The staff at Mount Pleasant Sunday school, c. 1920. It seems an extraordinary amount of staff to have for a Sunday school, but most children went to Sunday school in those days. The majority of parents, even if they were not particularly religious, regarded it as a matter of course. It also enabled the parents to have a little time to themselves.

six
Leisure

The police force marching down Queens Road past The Pilot pub as part of the Empire Day celebrations, 24 May 1912. Empire Day was a great occasion. Adults had the day off work and children the day off school. People used to wear a daisy in their buttonholes, because the British Empire had as many countries as the daisy has petals.

The procession celebrating King George V's Coronation passes along White Rock in June 1911. Buildings are decorated for the occasion. The banner on the left reads, 'Health, light and power to authority and peace and prosperity to the people.'

People have really gone to town with flags and bunting in Kings Road for the state visit of the Lord Mayor of London in 1908.

Crowds turn out to see the elephants marching two by two down Queens Road as the circus comes to town, *c.* 1900. Circuses continued to walk their elephants along the roads like this right up until the 1950s. The steeple in the background is St Andrew's church.

A regimental band marches down London Road followed by naval cadets. They are heading for Warrior Square. The clothes of the bystanders date it to the turn of the twentieth century, and the occasion is probably St George's Day.

The people riding in this splendid carriage are actually the staff of Hastings Gasworks, taking part in the Hastings Pageant of Heroes week, *c.* 1911. Behind them comes a float from one of the local churches.

Right: Jean Horsfall, Hastings Carnival Queen, 1949. This was the first carnival to be held since before the war.

Below: A magnificent pair of shire horses pull the Fremlin's float in the Hastings Carnival, 1962. Many residents felt that the carnival marginalized the Old Town, so in 1968 the Old Towners organized their own carnival, which became a highly successful annual event.

A special event draws the crowds in Alexandra Park, *c.* 1900. The lower end of the park was opened as St Andrew's Subscription Gardens in 1864. Further areas were added, and in 1878 the complete park was laid out by celebrated landscape designer Robert Marnock. It was formally opened by Edward VII and Queen Alexandra (then Prince and Princess of Wales) in 1882.

Visitors and residents listening to the band at the Alexandra Park bandstand, *c.* 1900. The bandstand was an original feature of the park when it opened, and has recently been splendidly restored by Hastings Borough Council as part of the park's regeneration programme.

'Come in number nine, your time is up!' Youngsters and adults alike enjoy the boating lake in Alexandra Park, *c*. 1907. The boating lake was created when the original St Andrew's Subscription Gardens were laid out in the early 1860s.

Three young ladies take a break from ice-skating to pose for the camera on Buckshole Reservoir at the top of Alexandra Park, *c*. 1910. Ice-skating was a very popular winter pastime in those days. This part of the park was added in 1872, shortly before it was landscaped by Marnock.

Families enjoying a day in St Leonards Gardens at the turn of the century. This was a favourite place for picnics; the two ponds, winding paths and uneven ground making it seem much larger than it is in reality.

An idyllic scene (though not for the fish!) taken at the height of summer, *c.* 1900. It is impossible to ascertain the location, but it is believed to be on the western outskirts of St Leonards.

Enjoying an energetic dance by the Fishmarket, *c.* 1900. It seems to be mostly women dancing together, a situation familiar to country dancers today.

A hot-air balloon is a major attraction at the fête held on the Central Cricket and Recreation Ground to celebrate the election of Sir Thomas Brassey as MP for Hastings, 1868.

The staff cricket team from the well-known Breeds Brewery, *c.* 1910. A.G. Taylor kneeling right. At the time this photograph was taken the bowling would have been underarm.

The Central Cricket Ground, around 1950, where many world-famous cricketers have played. Hastings, until recent years, cherished this first-class cricket ground, which was given to the town to be a green space in the town centre in perpetuity. However, the borough council built a shopping centre on it.

The bowling green in White Rock Gardens, *c.* 1930. The gardens were opened in 1926. The Falaise Hall (on the left) was opened for indoor bowls at the same time.

In the foreground is Holy Trinity church, with the memorial fountain to Countess Waldegrave in front, *c.* 1910. To its right, the beautiful building (like something out of Canaletto's Venice) is the Brassey Institute. Built 1878 by Sir Thomas Brassey, it was given by him to the town ten years later, to house the public library, museum, and School of Art & Science. He kept a private suite of rooms for his own use.

Children and adults alike enjoying a traditional Punch and Judy show on the beach, *c.* 1910. There seem to be no takers for the row of bathing machines lined up against the wall, although several people are in the water.

The flourishing and widely known Hastings Municipal Orchestra pose in front of the bandstand on Hastings Pier, 1921. On summers' evenings people could sit and listen, or just enjoy the music as they strolled along the promenade. In 1927 the orchestra moved into the newly built White Rock Pavilion.

The Salvation Army Band playing at White Rock, *c.* 1910. They were a familiar sight about the town. Their 'Iron Church' had been built in St Andrew's Square in 1865, and it remains there today. Behind them are the premises of White & Norton, the drapers.

Seen here in 1961, the Dolphin Jazz Band regularly played in the atmospheric surroundings of St Clements Caves, underneath the West Hill. During the war the caves were used as a massive air-raid shelter.

The 'Magpies' concert party, organized by Mrs Florence Kinder, around the time of the First World War. In the back row on the far left is Mrs Gladys Watson.

The White Rock Pavilion, seen here in the 1950s, was opened in 1927 by the Prince of Wales (later Edward VIII). It was a purpose-built home for the highly successful Hastings Municipal Orchestra, and also became a favourite venue for concerts and summer shows.

Queues waiting to see a show at the Gaiety Theatre in Queens Road, *c.* 1910. Doubtless the sweet shop next door did a roaring trade in 'finest confectionery' and 'high class chocolates'. The Gaiety opened in 1882 and featured many famous performers, such as Lillie Langtry. Gladstone addressed a meeting here in 1891, holding the stage for 1½ hours when he was in his eighties.

The Gaiety Theatre was converted into the Gaiety Cinema in 1932. There were at least seven cinemas in the town before the war, but the Gaiety, having undergone several changes of name, is the only one remaining. It is pictured here in 1978.

John Logie Baird demonstrating television to journalists in the 1920s. Baird carried out his experiments, not without some danger to his life, at his lodgings in Linton Crescent and his workshop in Queens Avenue. He succeeded in transmitting the flickering image of a Maltese Cross in 1924. Shortly afterwards he moved to London to get financial backing for his invention, returning to Bexhill at the end of his life

Baird's original television was made out of a tea chest, a biscuit tin, a 'bull's eye' lens and a toy electric motor. Unfortunately he had to sell it (for £2) to pay the rent. This early Baird television is in the Old Town Museum. It was quite possible for a knowledgeable amateur to make a television, and Baird's company sold DIY kits for the enthusiast.

seven

Transport

Above: A top-hatted coachman drives a boy and a dog in a carriage, accompanied by another boy on a bicycle, *c.* 1900. It is not known who these people are, but somebody has written the location 'Hollington' on the back of the photograph.

Right: Going on a day's outing in a horse-drawn charabanc, *c.* 1890. The vehicle is packed with passengers. It is at the height of summer and an awning protects the party from the heat.

The first motor vehicle to ply along the seafront, Good Friday, 1900. By the driver's left hand is a wonderful brass motor-horn with a rubber bulb on the end. The unprecedented event of a car motoring along the seafront made headline news in the *Hastings and St Leonards Observer*.

Several men study the impressive car at the by-election in 1908. Perhaps it has been used to convey voters in favour of Liberal candidate Mr Harcourt to the polling station. The posters on the wall read 'Last week Du Cros surprised Hastings! This week Hastings will surprise Du Cros!' William Harvey du Cros resigned as MP in that year, and the by-election was won by his son, Arthur.

Mr T.N. Ricklesford and his driver pose with the firm's carrier cart, based in Cambridge Gardens, *c*. 1895. A carrier would take anything from a parcel to a whole house of furniture.

Arthur Blackman's horse-drawn coal carts at his yard in Adelaide Road, *c*. 1900. He was a well-respected employer, and later became Mayor of Hastings several times. Blackman Avenue is named after him. His daughter Isabel was a great benefactor to the town.

A former stagecoach, probably on private hire, awaits its passengers outside Hastings Pier, *c.* 1900. The horses have their coats on until the vehicle is ready to start. The guard would stand on the platform at the back.

The Memorial – Hollington three-horse bus with its load of passengers, ready to start the return journey, *c.* 1900. Even at this early date the bus is carrying an advertisement, here for Nestles Milk [*sic*].

A well-matched team of dapple grey horses which must have looked splendid pulling the green bus. The passenger on the top deck looks affluent, as well he might, since the fares were extremely expensive. The bus belongs to the Hastings & St Leonards Omnibus Co. and is standing at Greenleaf Terrace, (now demolished), opposite the omnibus terminus at the Royal Albert pub, *c.* 1900.

Passengers board a motor bus belonging to the same company, plying between the Fishmarket and West Marina. The finely-proportioned Burton terrace to the left was later demolished to build Marine Court, *c.* 1910

Going out for a spin in a motor charabanc on a fine summers' day, *c.* 1920. Most of the women wear the fashionable cloche hats.

An old-fashioned Rambler coach waits at the Fishmarket to take visitors on a tour of the town, *c.* 1975. Behind is a more modern open-topped bus.

A top-hatted gentleman and a policeman watch labourers laying tramlines in London Road, 1905. Elegant ladies pick their way across the road works, in a scene reminiscent of Ford Madox Brown's painting, *Work*.

Laying tram lines at the junction of Hughenden Place and Mount Pleasant Road, 1905. It must have been a time of great chaos, with the roads all over the town being dug up at the same time. Trams met with much opposition when they first came to Hastings, but they soon replaced horse-buses.

Above: Boys run alongside the first tram as it passes through Silverhill Junction on its way to the town centre, 1905. The top deck is packed with a select company. Down at the Memorial hundreds of people were waiting to see it arrive.

Left: Archie Bryant, one of the first drivers employed by Hastings Tramways, poses proudly in his uniform by the gates of Beauport Park East Lodge, where he lived, 1905.

Left: Soldiers on Hastings tram No. 42 during the First World War. They were billeted in the town before going out to the Front. Note the female conductress, employed while the men were at the war.

Below: Trams on the sea-front, *c.* 1908. On the foremost tram the conductor is taking fares from the passengers on the upper deck. It is heading for West Marina, and advertises a local firm: 'Ask to be put down at Marriott's Photo Stores'. An early car is parked opposite.

Trolleybuses began operating in Hastings in 1928. This is one of the very first vehicles, standing at the reversing triangle where the wires ended by the Victoria Inn, Battle Road, *c*. 1935. The conductor is John Doyle.

Two single-deckers outside the White Rock Pavilion in the 1930s. Public transport was kept clean and shining in those days. The driver and conductor are wearing their white summer uniforms.

One of the new double-decker trolleybuses which came into service between 1940 and 1946. Although the war brought about a marked reduction in services, trolleybuses were well liked by their passengers, being cheap, efficient and reliable.

A down train is due at Hastings Railway Station, c. 1900. Several carriages wait in the forecourt, and a row of haulage vans with the horses in are ready for action. Meanwhile, two gardeners are watering the plants.

St Andrew's Archway shortly before it was demolished, c. 1898. This narrow road tunnel was so low that passengers on the upper deck of the horse-buses had to duck when passing through it.

The final moments of St Andrew's Archway under demolition in 1898. The present iron railway bridge was constructed in 1895 and the height of the railway embankment was increased at the same time.

One of the small steam railcars introduced on the Hastings–Ashford line in 1907. These allowed the opening of tiny halts going north-east from Hastings; Three Oaks, Doleham, and the now closed Snailham, used mainly by hop pickers.

A train pulls two carriages across the Crowhurst Viaduct high above the marshes, *c.* 1958. Known as the '17 Arches', this spectacular piece of railway architecture was blown up in 1969 after the Crowhurst to Bexhill branch line was closed.

eight

At War

What was the occasion, and were they in earnest or was it some sort of early re-enactment? The quality of the photographs suggests a date of around 1870.

These men look more like confederate soldiers from the American Civil War, but they are English and these two photographs were taken at Summerfields.

Right: A traditional Fishermen's Arch made to welcome the 4th Sussex Royal Volunteers at the end of the nineteenth century.

Below: Volunteers going out to fight in the Boer War pass through White Rock on their way to enlist at Shorncliffe, 1899. They are led by an artillery officer and make a stirring sight. The crowds have turned out to watch them.

As part of the 'Hastings Invasion' in 1909, Napier lorries line up in front of W & G du Cros Motorworks Ltd. A battalion of guards was sent from London to relieve the town from an imaginary invasion, as an experiment to see if motor vehicles could be used instead of horses for military transport.

The temporary war memorial at the bandstand in 1919. A nurse collects donations from passers-by for the War Memorial Fund. This is the same bandstand as the one on page 42.

The Earl of Cavan unveiling the permanent war memorial in Alexandra Park in 1922. Members of the armed forces are out in strength, and spectators line the far side of the boating lake on this moving occasion.

ARP wardens in May 1942. From left to right, back row: R. Barker, G. Hughes, S. Baker, E. Edwards, F.J. Sharley, A.G.M., W. McLean. Front row: L. Halger, J.H. Hornby, J. Parratt.

Above: Barbed wire was put all along the beach in 1940, stretching from the Old Town to Bo-Peep. People were forbidden to go on the beach, which was mined and sown with 'dragons' teeth'. Only a small segment of beach was left free for the fishing fleet to launch their boats. This photograph at Warrior Square also shows the bomb damage to Marine Court, 21 September 1942.

Left: A house in Nelson Road has its windows criss-crossed with sticky tape to prevent them being blown out by bomb blasts. As soon as war was declared, this became a common sight throughout the town, as householders prepared themselves for the worst.

Above: The old Swan Inn, High Street.
This ancient and famous coaching inn
was the hub of social life in the town in
early days. Demolished in 1889 and rebuilt
on the same site to a smaller scale, it was
bombed on 23 May 1943. As it was Sunday
lunchtime, it was crowded with locals and
there were many deaths. The site is now a
garden of remembrance to those who died.

Right: All Saints Street, 1945. Hastings took
a battering during the Second World War,
with a total of 550 HE (High Explosive)
bombs and fifteen flying bombs falling on
the town. One-hundred-and-fifty-four
people lost their lives and hundreds more
were injured. This derelict-looking scene
gives some idea of the aspect of the town
when peace finally came.

Other local titles published by Tempus

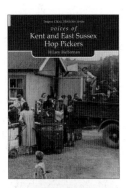

Voices of Kent and East Sussex Hop Pickers

HILARY HEFFERNAN

Right up to the late 1950s, the annual hop-picking season provided a welcome escape for thousands of families who lived and worked in the poorer parts of London, who would migrate every year to the hop gardens of Kent and Sussex to pick the harvest. The photographs and reminiscences in this book tell a fascinating story; of hardship, adventures, mishaps, misfortune and laughter experienced during hardworking holidays among the bines.

0 7524 3240 0

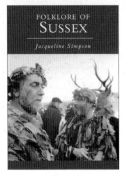

Folklore of Sussex

JACQUELINE SIMPSON

Sussex has a rich heritage of traditional local stories, customs and beliefs. Among the many topics explored in this volume are tales linked to landscape features and ancient churches which involve such colourful themes as lost bells, buried treasure, dragons, fairies and the devil. There are also traditions relating to ghosts, graves and gibbets and the strange powers of witches. Alongside the accounts of county customs are line drawings, photographs and printed ephemera relating to Sussex lore.

0 7524 2469 6

The Battle of Hastings 1066

M.K. LAWSON

1066 remains the most evocative date in English history: King Harold was defeated by William the Conqueror, and the rule of England passed abruptly from the control of Saxon to that of Norman kings. M.K. Lawson re-writes this pivotal turning point by subjecting the sources to the most detailed analysis ever undertaken. Illustrated with maps, battle plans and engravings of the Bayeux Tapestry, this book will hold its place as the most authoritative treatment of its subject for years to come.

0 7524 2689 3

Sussex CCC Greats

JOHN WALLACE

As cricket enters the twenty-first century, with its multitude of changes and initiatives, it seems appropriate to celebrate the lives of some of the men who have been part and parcel of the history of Sussex, the oldest of the county cricket clubs in this country. Since its formation in 1839, many Sussex players have brought great distinction to the game, on and off the field.

0 7524 2421 1

If you are interested in purchasing other books published by Tempus, or in case you have difficulty finding any Tempus books in your local bookshop, you can also place orders directly through our website

www.tempus-publishing.com